VISIONS
quilt expressions

edited by Stevii Thompson Graves

QUILT SAN DIEGO

RUTLEDGE HILL PRESS®
Nashville, Tennessee

**Library of Congress
Cataloging-in-Publication Data**

Visions: quilt expressions /
edited by Stevii Thompson Graves.
p.   cm.

Catalog of the sixth biennial exhibition of
Quilt San Diego to be held at the
Museum of San Diego History,
Nov. 7, 1998–Jan. 31, 1999.

ISBN 1-55853-678-7: (pbk.)

1. Quilts—United States—History
—20th century—Exhibitions.
I. Graves, Stevii Thompson.
II. Quilt San Diego (Organization)
III. Museum of San Diego History.
NK9112.V568   1998
746.46'074794'985—dc21   98—28584
CIP

Printed in China
1 2 3 4 5 6 7 8 9—00 99 98

Published by Rutledge Hill Press®,
211 Seventh Avenue North,
Nashville, Tennessee 37219.

Distributed in Canada by H. B. Fenn &
Company, Ltd., 34 Nixon Road, Bolton,
Ontario L7E 1W2.

Distributed in Australia by The Five Mile Press
Pty. Ltd., 22 Summit Road, Noble Park,
Victoria 3174.

Distributed in New Zealand by Tandem Press,
2 Rugby Road, Birkenhead, Auckland 10.

Distributed in the United Kingdom by
Verulam Publishing, Ltd., 152a Park Street
Lane, Park Street, St. Albans, Hertfordshire
AL2 2AU.

Cover and page design by
Anderson Thomas Design, Nashville, TN

Typesetting by John Mitchell, Nashville, TN

We define a work of art as a work which is in some way extraordinary. It is expressive and invites us to see ourselves and the world anew or inspires us in a new way.

We want the best in quiltmaking today. It is certainly not our intention to simply shock the public. While it is important to represent the range of today's quiltmaking, it is equally important that each quilt possess a vitality of its own and be able to stand alone as well as work together with the other quilts to provide an exhibition that somehow "jells" together.

We want the public to see a range of quilts, some which perhaps may initially "feel" familiar and also those that will make viewers stop and think, evoke an emotion, have an opinion. We want quilts that derive from the necessity to communicate—that speak from the soul of the quiltmaker.

We want quilts that flow with color, sparkle with excitement, those that make visual impacts, and those that are so subtle that one must look closely to see unusual use of fabric, high technical skills, and other marvelous effects used to create the design.

We want all those wonderful, incredible quilts that express the quiltmaker's creativity. We want an exhibit that compels the viewer to return for more than one look.

Joan F. Austin

Juror's Statement

Joan F. Austin is the head of the Textiles and Weaving programs at San Diego State University, School of Art, Design, and Art History. She has been teaching at the university for 28 years. Joan is an artist whose work is featured in many publications and museums.

The 1998 Visions exhibition is the result of a mind-boggling amount of preparation accomplished through great teamwork by the membership of Quilt San Diego, one of the best organized and most enthusiastic groups I've ever met. I want to thank their members and especially Merilyne J. Hickman, President for this year's exhibition, for inviting me to participate as one of the jurors. It has been an honor to work with my fellow jurors Libby Lehman and Robert Shaw, whom I admire and respect for the wealth of knowledge they possess.

Our mission as jurors was to choose an exhibition limited to 80 quilts. Each of the 895 entries was studied and then the selection began. The strength of the works that were chosen was their commitment to a focused idea and an overall strong vision. Subtle or bold, these quilts had a sense of totality that expressed clarity of idea and strong composition. They mirrored completeness.

The makers of the selected quilts are obviously masters of every aspect of the process, from concept to resolution of the finest detail. They take their work seriously. Artists new to this endeavor will find rich historical and contemporary art quilt tradition to inspire their quilting experiences. Great quilts are worth studying carefully for insight both into design and into craft technology. There is more to making quilts than repeating the tried and tested historical form. It is the small complexities that make new variations possible. Dedicated hard work by serious artists advances the need to question the directions of current expression in the field and will continue to lead us to make new discoveries and further enrich the quilt dialogue. Most artists tend to find their own paths to the unexpected possibilities, paths that are located in the tiny cracks left unexplored or the gaping holes where opportunities await inventive souls to add their measure of uniqueness.

In this age of new technology and fast-paced life styles, quiltmaking seems to embody the gentleness that nurtures and rebuilds the human spirit. Why is the stitching together of bits of cloth so significant for us today? It is a visual record of time and human accomplishment, and quilting is for many a meditative visual language. It is the voice of reason in a chaotic society. It is a metaphor for mending and making right the outside world. In its most basic meaning, it is creating with love and patience treasures for the future. It is the work of the artist who desires to pursue a path of decision-making that resolves an idea, who concentrates on perfecting appropriate technical processes, and who leads the way to expressive and intelligent art. Experimentation, risk, and challenge are rewarded with work that contributes to the field. It will be exhibitions such as Visions that continue to showcase and sustain this important textile art tradition.

Libby Lehman

Juror's Statement

There are three rules for making a successful quilt.
Unfortunately, nobody knows what they are.

— paraphrase of Somerset Maugham

Entering Visions takes at least one quilt, a little money, some courage and a lot of hope. Getting accepted is more complicated. It is always a chancy endeavor, subject to more variables than a rocket launch. Many factors go into selecting the final 80 quilts. As a juror there are certain things I look for in a quilt:

Something that makes me want to see it again. This can be any number of things, from elegant design to funky embellishments, fresh color combinations to innovative techniques. Katie Pasquini Masopust's *Passage — Chaco* made me want to look at it again and again. I feel that there are still things I can discover in it even after multiple viewings.

Artistic integrity. Every part of the quilt should be there for a reason and contribute to a unified whole. Liz Axford combines materials and design in *Emotions & Abstractions 4* so that all the elements complement each other.

Originality combined with mastery. Vita Marie Lovett's *Primitive Door Series VI — Mary's Barn* is a fresh design beautifully executed.

Good photography. Overall, the quality of the slides we viewed was very good. A clear and accurate image is vital to the selection process.

After considering all of this, I was more than satisfied with the quilts chosen for Visions: Quilt Expressions. I feel they ably represent the healthy, burgeoning art quilt movement we are currently experiencing.

It is a pleasure to be involved in the jurying of Visions: Quilt Expressions. I would like to thank Merilyne Hickman and her committee for their assistance, and my fellow jurors for their expertise and camaraderie. Enjoy the show.

Libby Lehman is a studio art quiltmaker from Houston, Texas. She has taught and lectured extensively throughout the United States as well as Japan, Australia, New Zealand, Germany, and Switzerland. Her prize-winning quilts are in many private, museum and corporate collections. She was named by Nihon Vogue *as one of the 88 Leaders in today's quilt world. Libby has juried and judged for Quilt National '95, American International Quilt Association, Quilter's Heritage, and many others. Her latest book,* Threadplay, *was released in October 1997.*

Robert Shaw

Juror's Statement

Robert Shaw is one of the country's leading authorities on American crafts and folk arts and the author of the acclaimed books Quilts: A Living Tradition, Hawaiian Quilt Masterpieces, America's Traditional Crafts, *and* The Art Quilt. *The former curator of the Shelburne Museum in Vermont, he is now a consultant to collectors and museums nationwide.*

Jurying a respected international competition like Quilt San Diego's Visions is a great honor and privilege. As jurors of this year's competition, Libby Lehman, Joan Austin, and I knew we could look forward to seeing wonderful quilts by some of the best artists at work in this field today and that we could expect to be introduced to exciting work by new and completely unfamiliar artists. But while we could anticipate considerable pleasure, jurying a show of this stature is also a serious responsibility. As jurors we were entrusted with the job of choosing 80 quilts of the "highest aesthetic and artistic quality" from a field of close to 900 entries by 544 different artists, and we were expected to bring the sum of our experience and knowledge as curators, artists, teachers, and scholars to that solemn task.

The competition among entrants was strong, and a number of worthy quilts inevitably had to be left out of the exhibition. We jurors appreciated the deeply personal risk that the hundreds of entrants had taken in putting their work before us, knowing as they did from the outset that we would have to disappoint 85% of them. We therefore approached our work deliberately and with the most careful attention we could muster. Since it was impossible to see the quilts in person, we juried them by looking at slides projected in a dark room, a poor second to physical examination at best. In many if not most cases, we had never actually seen the quilt we were looking at, so we tried hard to move beyond the illusion of the projected slide image and realize we were viewing a three-dimensional textile, not a flat piece of art. We did our best to visualize the actual quilt, consider the quality of its workmanship, savor its stuffed and quilted textures, and imagine its size and physical impact when hung in the exhibition space. Although we could sometimes guess, we didn't know whose work we were looking at, only the name of the quilt, its dimensions, materials, and construction details. We were also ignorant of the artists' explanations of their own work that accompany the photographs in this catalog. Our judgments were thus restricted to visual and aesthetic criteria.

So then, you might ask, what is a juror seeking as he or she looks through nearly 900-odd sets of slides? Here I have to speak for myself, as I'm sure Libby and Joan, my partners in this enterprise, will also want to do. First of all, a successful entry has to make an immediate impression on me. It needs to distinguish itself from the pack and grab my attention in some way. It also needs to have the power to hold my interest, to make me want to come back to it again, to offer something different and richer with each viewing. I want to be delighted, challenged, surprised, puzzled, moved, or amused by what I see. I want to see something I haven't seen before—quilts that ignore trends and that I can't trace directly to origins in a well-known teacher's workshop or another artist's stylistic vocabulary or bag of tricks. Most of all, I want to see quilts that have an integrity of their own, that project a singular, fresh, and original point of view, that speak with their own voice, clearly and directly.

Because I'm also charged with putting together an exhibition, I want to choose a group of quilts that will complement each other, whose whole is somehow greater than the sum of its parts. I want to choose many different types of quilts: I hope to find interesting examples of wholecloth, pieced, and appliquéd work; to include painted, dyed, photo-transferred and embellished quilts; to show pattern variations that breathe new life into traditional themes as well as exciting new designs that take quilts someplace they have never been before. I want to gather an engaging mix of big, enveloping quilts and jewel-like miniatures; graphic abstracts and realistic pictorials; quilts of great technical complexity and quilts of powerful simplicity; quilts with bold color juxtapositions and quilts of the most evanescent hues; assertive quilts that immediately "knock my socks off" and quiet quilts that slowly but inexorably draw me in to reveal their secrets. I think most, if not all, of those elements are represented here, and I believe that the exhibition we have chosen offers a rich slice of the diverse work currently being done by quilt virtuosos around the world. I hope you will enjoy experiencing these quilts, whether in person or only through this catalog, as much as I and my fellow jurors have enjoyed selecting them for you.

In closing, I want to thank the board of Quilt San Diego for inviting me to help jury and to give my special thanks to Quilt San Diego's seemingly indefatigable and unflappable President, Merilyne Hickman, for making my stay in San Diego such a pleasure. Thanks also to Merilyne and our hardworking scribe, Julie Zglinick, for treating me to a wonderful day at the San Diego Zoo, to all the Quilt San Diego board and staff members for making the jurying process run so smoothly, and to Libby and Joan for their expertise and insight and for being so much fun to work with.

Quilts Japan Prize Nihon Vogue sponsored the Quilts Japan Prize for the 1994 and 1996 Visions exhibitions and will provide another Quilts Japan Prize to a Visions 1998 artist. The recipient of the 1998 award is Liz Axford of Houston, Texas. The objective of the Quilts Japan Prize is to express gratitude for the continued growth of the Japanese quilt, which is due greatly to American quilters, and to pay respect to the predecessors of quiltmaking. With this award, Nihon Vogue hopes to play a role in the development of quiltmaking by helping to link the ties between Japanese and American quiltmakers.

Penny Nii Art Quilt Award Penny Nii, the owner of Penny Nii Art Quilt, has sponsored this award since the Visions 1996 exhibition to encourage the artists that work in this medium that allows them to work in a mixture of traditional techniques, designs, and materials. The contemporary art quilt has become a unique art form. The winning quilt was selected by the three Visions jurors for its artistic merit. The recipient of this award is Katie Pasquini-Masopust of Santa Fe, New Mexico. It is hoped that the award will help artists focus on the art components of composition and color in addition to traditional craftsmanship and techniques.

The Rookie Award Studio Art Quilt Associates, a non-profit national organization, was founded to serve artists working in the quilt medium whose work deserves the recognition of collectors and dealers who tend to invest in artists whose commitment, growth, and originality is proven by a body of work known to them. The organization also serves dealers, teachers, curators, and collectors who recognize the importance of the emerging art quilt but need to know more about the field's depth and range. To facilitate their goal, Studio Art Quilt Associates is offering for the first time The Rookie Award to recognize a "newcomer" to the Visions exhibition. Visions: Quilt Expressions is featuring 47 first-time Visions exhibitors in the 1998 exhibition. The Board of Directors of Quilt San Diego was asked to select the recipient of this award. Their choice was based on artistic merit, technique, and overall impression. Visions artist Vita Marie Lovett of Marietta, Georgia, was selected to be the recipient of the award. Her work is entitled *Primitive Door Series VI — Mary's Barn*.

President's Choice Award Canyon Quilters of San Diego is a non-profit organization established in 1985 to meet the needs and desires of local quilters living in San Diego County who wanted to share their love for quilting with others. The Guild enjoys a membership of approximately 250 individuals and offers a monthly meeting and speaker's program for its members.

In an effort to acknowledge the importance that Quilt San Diego and the presentation of the biennial Visions exhibition represent to the San Diego area quilters, the Guild is sponsoring for the first time the President's Choice Award. The recipient of the award is selected by the President of Quilt San Diego. The President has based her choice on the quilt in the exhibition which she personally finds the most exciting in color, technique, and workmanship. Her decision was difficult because all the quilts in Visions: Quilt Expressions are excellent; however, only one could be selected. Visions artist Jan Rickman of Whitewater, Colorado, has been selected to be the recipient of the award. Her work is entitled *Close Encounter*.

Sponsors *Quilt San Diego received significant help from these corporate sponsors in producing this catalog and the exhibition. We are very grateful for their financial assistance and their continued interest in promoting the quilt as art.*

Rosie's Calico Cupboard Quilt Shop, San Diego California *Catering to quilters and crafters since 1983. Offering more than 8,000 bolts of first quality 100% cotton fabrics. Classes and an extensive selection of notions, books, and patterns are also available. Located at 7151 El Cajon Boulevard, San Diego, California.*

Friends of Fiber Art International *An organization whose purpose is to increase the appreciation and understanding of contemporary art in fibrous materials. Disseminates information about and encourages the collection of contemporary fiber art, supports museum shows of fiber art through funding, supports fiber art exhibitions in galleries, and is involved in many other activities related to the fiber arts.*

Bernina Corporation *Bernina of America, Inc., is the U.S. distributor of Swiss Bernina and Bernette Sewing Machines, embroidery machines, overlock machines, machine accessories, and educational products. Distributors in the San Diego area are: Bits & Pieces, Escondido; La Mesa Sew & Vac, La Mesa; Sew Much Better, Encinitas; and Sew Hut, San Diego.*

21st Century Bob *Trading in items of unusual interest and lasting value; Italian motorcycles, textiles, primitive, found and folk art, old tools, belt driven machinery, and more. Located at 1205 J Street, San Diego, California.*

Husqvarna Viking Sewing Machine Company, Bazaar del Mundo, Gay Sinclair, Nihon Vogue, Penny Nii Art Quilt, Studio Art Quilt Associates, Canyon Quilters of San Diego, Omnigrid, Inc., Fairfield Processing, Zook's Warehouse for Quilters, Friendship Quilters, Robert Kaufman Company, Seaside Quilters of San Diego, *Art Quilt Magazine*, and Springs Industries.

Quilt San Diego is proud to celebrate the presentation of its sixth biennial exhibition, Visions: Quilt Expressions, at the Museum of San Diego

History from November 7, 1998, through January 31, 1999. Since the debut of the first exhibition in 1987, the organization has developed and carefully nurtured a distinguished reputation as an international arts organization dedicated to the promotion and appreciation of the quilt as art. Over the years, our excellent reputation has continually grown in stature. We are proud of our growth and continued influence in the promotion of the recognition of the quilt as an art form.

A non-profit organization, Quilt San Diego depends heavily on its volunteers to keep the everyday activities and production work for Visions operating. Our membership, corporate sponsors, and grant benefactors have helped support the organization through financial assistance, enabling us to continue our operations and achieve our goals. Without the dedication and hard work of individuals, corporations, organizations, and the artists who continue to produce exceptional art quilts, Quilt San Diego and Visions would not have achieved the prestige it enjoys today.

Acknowledgments

In recognition and appreciation of those who have assisted Quilt San Diego and contributed to its success and continued growth, I extend my sincere thanks to:

The members of the Board of Directors of Quilt San Diego: Gay Sinclair, Lois Hammond, JoDee Arnold, Julia Zgliniec, and Lynn Glynn.

The Quilt San Diego Advisory Board: Michael James, Penny McMorris, David Walker, Sharyn Craig, Jean Ray Laury, and Will Chandler.

Former members of the Board of Directors of Quilt San Diego: Diane Seaberg, Karen Emberton, Debby Timby, Patty Garretson, Maggie McKerrow, Shirlee Smith, Cynthia Hansen, Pat Marean, Lynn Johnson, Kate Besser, Carol O'Brien, Karen Wooten, Linda Hamby, Sharyn Craig, Arlene Stamper, Patty Smith, Rose Turner, Alice Busse, Barbara Hartung, Shirley Grear, Judy Hopkins, Christen Brown, Martha Ehringer, Stevii Graves, LeeAnn Decker, Janet Rogers, Lucinda Eddy, Karen Bowden, Linda Gruber, Cecilia Stanford, Suzanne Appelman, and Jean Benelli

Jurors for Visions: Quilt Expressions: Robert Shaw, Libby Lehman, and Joan Austin

Editor for the 1998 catalog, *Visions: Quilt Expressions*: Stevii Thompson Graves

Visions Committee Chairpersons: JoDee Arnold, Lynn Glynn, Julia Zgliniec, Lois Hammond, Gay Sinclair, Phyllis Newton, Kay Lettington, Patti Sevier, and Stevii Graves

Our membership, corporate sponsors, and the many volunteers who have given their time, money, and support

Bob and Gay Sinclair for their generosity and assistance to Quilt San Diego

Friends of Fiber Art International for a generous grant to help finance the catalog

The San Diego Historical Society and the Museum of San Diego History for providing a museum setting for the exhibition and providing assistance throughout the production and presentation of Visions: Quilt Expressions

Rutledge Hill Press for publishing our 1998 catalog, *Visions: Quilt Expressions*

Carina Woolrich Photography for the excellent photography she has consistently provided.

And most of all, Quilt San Diego wishes to recognize and express its appreciation for the wonderful contributions of all the artists featured in previous Visions exhibitions and especially this year's exhibition and the artists who entered their quilts for our jurying process. Without their "visions," expressed through their creations and implemented through the quilt in an art form, there would be no growth in the development of the art quilt. Quilt San Diego is proud to be an important avenue in inspiring and displaying that growth.

Merilyne J. Hickman
President, Board of Directors
Quilt San Diego

VISiONS

quilt expressions

Urban Flight is the product of my search for innovation in quilt subject matter and conceptual ideas. Its immediate inspiration was photographs of distorted images of neighboring buildings reflected in the ubiquitous glass and steel buildings of modern cities. Also, I am struck by the concept of central cities as aviaries. Imagine a giant invisible cage enclosing the city and all the creatures in it. People may enter and leave the cage at will; the birds do not appear to do so.

The flying shapes were created by tucking the fabric before pressing the transferred images of San Francisco, Chicago, Athens, and Istanbul. After pressing, the fabric was untucked to reveal the "ghost" birds, flying free from the tightly controlled arrangement of tessellated images.

Notwithstanding the title of the quilt, no political statement is intended.

Deborah Melton Anderson

Columbus, Ohio

Urban Flight
31.50″ x 26.75″

Cotton twill, cotton flannel batting, cotton threads

Photo heat transfers on tucked cotton twill, colored pencil, machine quilted

Cheri Arnold

Dublin, Ohio

Twisted in Texas
48" x 69"

*Commercial and hand-dyed cotton fabrics, textile
paints, fusible web, embroidery floss*

*Machine and hand pieced, machine and
hand appliquéd, machine quilted,
airbrushed, and stamped*

Lady Bird, Lady Bird,
Fly Away Home!
Your House is on Fire,
Your Children are Gone...

This simple Mother Goose rhyme kept sneaking into my mind as I put
Twisted in Texas together—a haunting metaphor for what I was feeling.
This quilt is about fractured families and childhood innocence gone up
in flames.

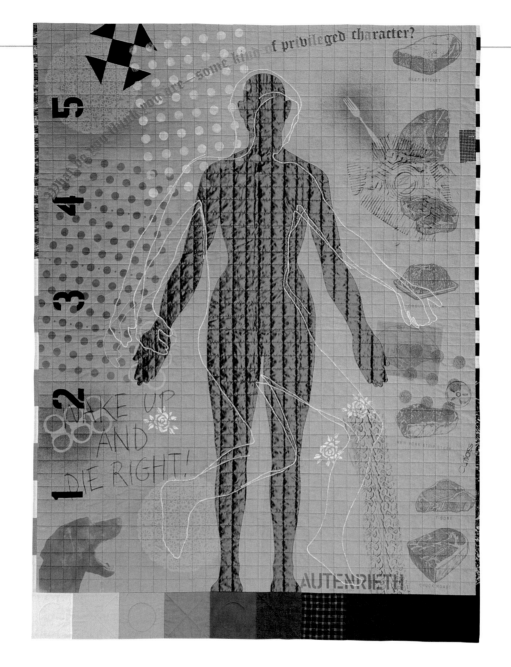

This is a pastiche of dreams, memories, ruminations, and fantasies accompanying the theme of the double, and as such, a continuation of my current preoccupation with the self. It is also a collaboration with the anonymous makers of many of the images, including the traditional Shoo-fly pattern "flying" across the top and the human figure template blown up to life size.

Patricia Autenrieth

Hyattsville, Maryland

Doppelgänger

56" x 74"

Cottons, blends, taffeta, photo dye, spray enamel, fabric paint and crayon

Hand appliquéd, machine quilted

13

Liz Axford

Houston, Texas

**Emotions and
Abstractions 4**

70″ x 50″

*Hand-dyed cotton broadcloth, commercial
discharged fabrics*

*Immersion dyed, shibori dyed, hand painted,
discharge dyed, machine pieced, machine quilted*

Quilts Japan Prize Winner

In the winter of 1997 my mother died. In the weeks preceding and
following her death, it seemed that every experience we ever shared,
every conversation we'd ever had, came flooding back. It was
overwhelming. I knew I would turn to this series to sort things out.

The following summer my husband and I visited our good friends Janet
and Don Steadman at their home overlooking Useless Bay on Whidbey
Island, Washington. One afternoon we walked out on the beach during
low tide. Embossed in the sand was the pattern of the waves retreating,
sometimes accented with seaweed, sometimes punctuated with shells.
Sometimes a small rivulet of running water broke the relentless pattern
of the waves.

This quilt is dedicated to the memory of my mom.

In this quilt, images of grasses, birds, and animals are in motion expressing change. Their nature is as transient as our memories and our lives.

Roxana Bartlett

Boulder, Colorado

If Recollecting Were Forgetting

67" x 67"

Cotton canvas, sateen, velvet, Procion dye, acrylic paint

Pieced, dyed, painted, tied with perle cotton

Elizabeth Barton

Athens, Georgia

Goodramgate

66″ x 53″

Cotton fabric, dyed, screen-printed and painted fabric

Appliquéd, pieced, and quilted

Goodramgate is the name of a street in my hometown of York, England. This quilt has layers of meanings for me.

First: the scene, the haphazard beauty of the medieval houses, jumbled, creaking and bowed, full of history, character and light.

Second: as age overtakes, to appreciate the mellowing of nature.

Third: memories of home, the past, the people, the rose gardens.

Fourth: thoughts of roads not taken, what might have been, and what has been.

Fifth: the persistence of memory, time past, and time future within time present.

In 1985, while visiting the Print and Textile Study Room of the Dallas Museum of Art, I was able to privately view two raffia skirts made by the Kuba people of the Congo. Later the Kuba skirts were put on public display at the museum. Seeing them mounted in their entire length renewed my interest, and I began working on a series based on the overall form and construction of the skirts as the appliqué patterning. That was in January 1992, the month my father died.

This series is in remembrance of my father, Milt Benner, and also in praise of these exquisite textiles, the ceremonial skirts of the Kuba. The titles of all six—*Memory, Tribute, Honor, Respect, Character,* and *Reverence*—reflect an aspect of homage to a person and to a people's traditional art form.

Sue Benner

Dallas, Texas

Reverence: Kuba Skirt Series VI

120″ x 41″

Dye on silk, commercial silk, cotton, rayon and metallic thread

Dye painted, immersion dyed, shibori, fusing, machine quilted and constructed

17

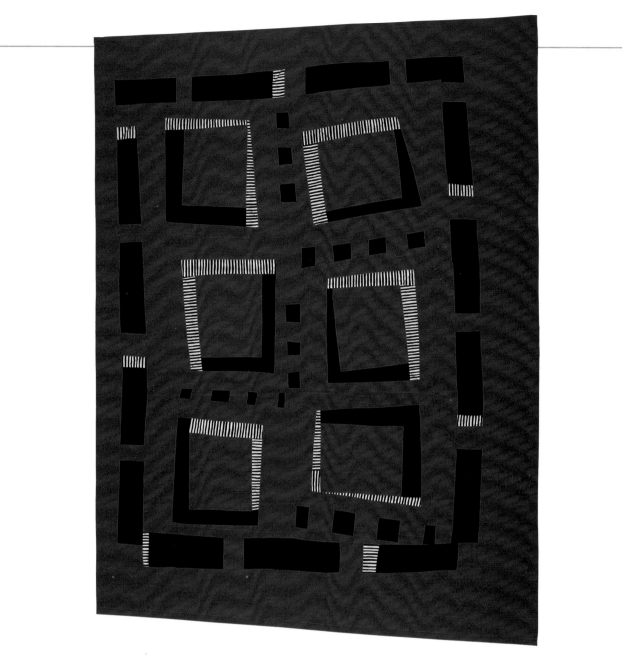

Charlotte S. Bird

San Diego, California

Epicenter

29" x 40"

Commercial cotton, cotton batting, polyester thread

Freehand cut, machine pieced, machine quilted

On a wedding anniversary not long ago, I awoke in our cabin feeling like a bubble in a can of paint vibrating in a hardware store. Twelve tons of rock had cascaded down a cliff I planned to climb. This quilt began as a color exercise on my worktable. As it grew, I saw the core of the seismic waves and the swarms of aftershocks that wiggle Southern California's mountains. A critic I respect reminds me never to trust an artist's understanding of her own work.

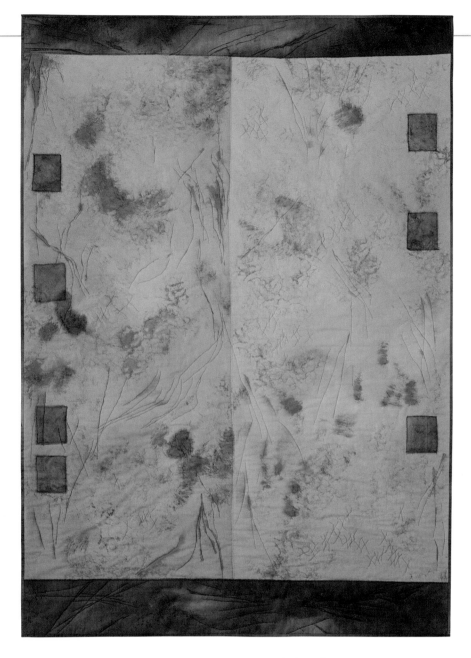

This work developed out of a personal history of creating artwork that addresses structure, growth and connections through surfaces composed of small, torn squares and rectangles. The emphasis in my current work is on the painted surface versus directing the work through construction methods. Simple structure is balanced with painted and stitched surfaces, allowing the elements of simplicity and complexity to coexist. *Flow IV* suggests the give-and-take approach to living life, an approach both strong and fragile.

Erika Carter

Bellevue, Washington

Flow IV

39" x 54"

Cotton fabric, silk organza, cotton machine embroidery thread

Hand painted, direct machine appliquéd, machine quilted and hand stitched

Violet O. Cavazos

Falls Church, Virginia

Girafics

73" x 83"

Screen-printed cotton fabric, cotton prints and solids, cotton batting

Machine pieced, machine quilted and hand quilted with perle cotton

While browsing for fabric, I was attracted to a bold, graphic Marimekko screen-printed remnant. I soon became obsessed and fascinated with incorporating the graphic design with constructed pieces resembling graphics. Fortunately, after completing the quilt top, I was able to purchase additional yardage for backing and more graphic designed fabric for the next quilt in the series.

A New Day came from the idea of pots. In every society, each new day is started with a pot, whether it be a pot to make coffee or tea, one to fetch water, or one to prepare breakfast.

I saw many shapes and sizes of handmade pots while living in Africa. A woman's life revolves around these pots. They are an essential part of her everyday routine.

The design of the quilting and the placement of the African fabrics come from the ellipses of the pots in this quilt.

Hollis Chatelain

Hillsborough, North Carolina

A New Day
45" x 48"

Cotton fabric, Procion dyes, Prismacolor pencils, Krylon fixative, African-made fabrics, Madeira threads

Double-dyed cotton fabric with and without resists, highlighted with Prismacolor pencils, machine quilted

Jane Burch Cochran

Rabbit Hash, Kentucky

A Quilt for the Child
I Never Had

55″ x 39″

*Fabric, beads, buttons, found objects
(including a child's dress, crocheted flowers
and leaves, doilies, old needle case, etc.)
etching inks and paint*

*Machine pieced, hand appliquéd using
beads, photocopy transfers of fortunes, quilted
with embroidery thread, buttons and beads*

I have done four quilts using a baby's or a small child's dress. This is the last in the series for now. I took a monoprint class and used the dress as a plate by first coating it with acrylic medium and running it through the printing press between wax paper to flatten it. I made a couple of prints on paper. Since my art mind-set is "quilt," I liked the look of the dress with the etching ink on it and the contrast provided by the red brocade. I envisioned sewing the gold beads in random curling lines. It was going to be a quick quilt, but as usual, I got carried away. I love doing the patchwork border, including a few old quilt squares and xeroxed fortunes, then added the crocheted flowers and leaves plus other found objects, including an old needle case turned backwards and a strange aluminum "something" I picked up off the ground at Penland School a couple of years ago. I am trying to push embellishment, to include more found objects and things I have not used before. The title came to me and I realized that this was what the quilt was.

The Tangerine Tango was the result of a playful painting and quilting session done to music. The mind-set working with the concept: the less planning and preconceived notions, the more the improvisational spirit comes through; the more spontaneous and surprising this language of shapes and color can be; the more the creative process itself is enjoyed.

Meredyth Colberg

Fox River Grove, Illinois

The Tangerine Tango
23″ x 22″

Screen-printing ink, Melody Johnson's hand-dyed cotton thread, purchased rayon thread

Screen printed, free-motion embroidered and quilted, hand embroidered

Sharon Meares Commins

Los Angeles, California

Exuberance

30″ x 50″

Cotton, cotton and rayon threads

Dye painting of both fabric and some of the larger threads, appliquéd, free-motion machine quilted, original machine lace technique used to edge the heart shapes

This one is for my free-spirited daughter, who leads with her heart.

Along the marshes of the Northern California coast, channels of isolated beauty reflect the changing face of the sky along their path to the sea. *Estuario* celebrates the preservation of these waterways whose existence supports an amazing variety of plant and animal life that has adapted to the challenges of life along these tidal waters, areas not always thought worthy of protection.

The name *Estuario* (Spanish for estuary) refers to early Spanish visitors who recorded their impressions of coastal California through the poetry of their language. Design inspiration for *Estuario* was derived from colorful stripes of the Latin American serape, a symbolic reference to a warm, woven blanket whose inherent purpose is protection from the outside world.

Judith Content

Palo Alto, California

Estuario

70″ x 55″

Thai silk, silk satin, silk noil, poly-cotton batting, poly-cotton thread

Hand-dyed silk using Japanese shibori technique "bomaki," pieced and quilted

Sandi Cummings

Moraga, California

Cold Winter Quilt II

50.5″ x 44.5″

*Screen-printed and hand-dyed cotton fabric,
commercial fabric, perle cotton #8*

*Machine pieced, machine appliquéd and
embroidered, machine quilted*

This is second in a series of abstract landscape quilts combining
elements of earth substrata and surface features.

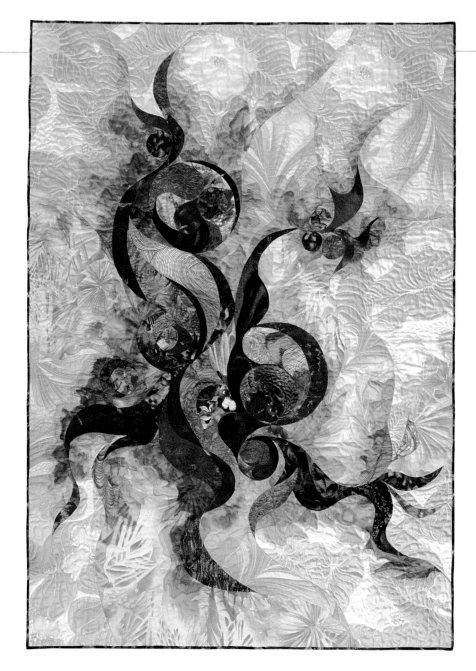

This quilt is the third in my series of Fantasy Form designs derived from a number of doodles done mostly "in flight." The drawings come quite directly from the subconscious, and the imagery is a symptom of my current obsession with anything round—grapes, marbles, antique glass floats, planets—which I choose not to analyze too closely.

Judy B. Dales

Kingwood, Texas

Dancing on the Dark Side of the Moon

40" x 60"

Cotton, poly cotton, chiffon, tulle, cotton batting

Machine pieced, appliquéd, quilted and hand appliquéd

Deanna M. Davis

Piedmont, California

Scenic Byways #3–6

55″ x 40″

Hand-dyed cotton and silk fabrics, commercial cotton and polyesters, silk and rayon thread

Raw-edge appliqué, straight and satin stitch top stitching, fused appliqué

Finally, I have learned to be comfortable with the fact that I may not be able to put words to my pieces for a very long time but that I will come to understand them.

Scenic Byways is a series studying space and relationships.

#3–6 examine the strength and beauty of the individual while celebrating the whole.

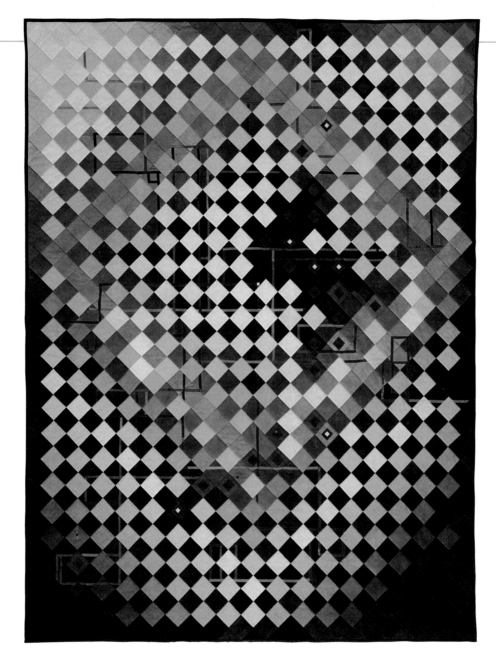

Red Leaves is one of a series in which space and dimension are explored by defining planes at various depths. I strive for a sense of rhythm and harmony in these abstract images while attempting to maintain parsimony of palette and simplicity of construction. Water is a natural subject because of the contrast between reflected light and the dark, meditative allure of the depths. This image was inspired by the black waters of a stream reflecting a white autumn sky. Leaves float downstream and lie submerged with rocks and branches.

Catherine Dawson

Calais, Maine

Red Leaves Drift Downstream

50.5″ x 67.5″

Hand-dyed cotton fabric, commercial cotton binding, Fairfield Cotton Classic batting

Machine pieced, machine quilted, fused details

Jo Diggs

Portland, Maine

Remembered Vistas

64.5" x 48.5"

Cotton and assorted fabrics

Hand appliquéd, pieced, hand quilted

Remembered Vistas continues the exploration of two ongoing themes: views across a wide valley toward mountains, and multiple views of landscapes in one quilt. Hand-painted and hand-dyed fabrics are used for the most dramatic light and color effects and are integrated with many layers of commercial fabrics. This quilt pays homage to the beauty of earth and sky.

Untitled #2 is part of a series of pieces that rely on clues and inspirations observed in nature. Green leaves with purple veins, orange cosmos blooming alongside lavender and the sinewy line drawn by red yuccas in both flower and foliage are some of the many lessons harvested from my garden and applied in my image-making.

Malka Dubrawsky

Austin, Texas

Untitled #2

31″ x 39″

Hand-dyed and discharged pima cotton, cotton batting

Machine pieced, machine quilted

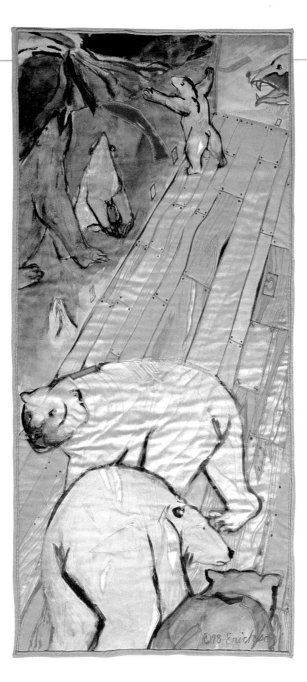

Nancy N. Erickson

Missoula, Montana

Hall of Memory #3: Seeking Re-entry

27" x 58.25"

Cottons, velvets, satin, pearlescent paint, charcoal, pencil and paintstick

Machine appliquéd and quilted, painted

Hall... alludes to the mystery and spiritual aura of the early cave drawings. The time is in the future. The bears come upon a deserted human residence covered with drawings of bear history; they wonder at the events shown just as we do know, and they are confined, just as early people crawling through narrow passages into ancient caves were.

I purchased the book *Dawn of Art: The Chauvet Cave* as I made this particular quilt and am reading it and still working with this theme, now amplified by new publications and enriched by old ones (such as *On the Track of Prehistoric Man*, read 30 years ago). Nothing is very clear in direction here. I just keep experimenting with techniques and learning from piece to piece.

In *Green Tea* my intention was to create a fluid form of expression by combining traditional textiles with painting and surface manipulation. The color and topography of the natural landscape played a large part in my choice of surface colors and textures.

Suzan Friedland

San Francisco, California

Green Tea
140″ x 90″

Linen, cotton, acrylic

Hand painted, machine quilted

Britt Friedman

Oberlin, Ohio

Radiance

53" x 72"

Transparent fabric paints, cotton sateen, cotton batting, cotton canvas, thread

Hand painted with transparent fabric paints on white cotton sateen, machine quilted

After making a series of quilts where I tried to push the idea of asymmetry as far as possible, I decided to try the opposite: creating a series of quilts that would have motion and liveliness while retaining their symmetrical aspects. These quilts vary in their abstractions but all have designs derived from nature. In this work I have tried to make a visually interesting quilt which also shares the qualities of warmth, spiritually, and community with the viewer.

Even though fabric is my medium, I still consider myself a painter-draftsman. I also use transparent materials which act as glazes. The thread of the embroidery creates contour lines when needed, and I use scattered pieces of fabric along with fast-drying acrylic paint to give the work a painterly effect. The patterns of the fabric are highlighted by the painterly brush strokes and the design combines the flat abstract shapes with the representational voluminous apples.

Leslie Gabrielse

Rotterdam, The Netherlands

Goblet I

76" x 61"

Cotton and other fabrics, yarn, acrylic paints

Appliquéd by hand with yarn

Margie Garratt

Constantia, South Africa

Lost in Time – A South American Experience

33″ x 42.5″

Hand-dyed and commercial fabrics, tweed fabrics

Machine pieced, machine and hand quilted

My family and I spent two months exploring parts of South America, taking particular interest in the history and anthropology of the continent. Traveling with my family tends to be a quite physically demanding experience, with all 80 km of the Inca Trail up and down the spine of the Andes being just one of the challenges that faced me. I loved the continent, photographed and read widely, and on my return I was intent on expressing some of the magic I had experienced.

I assembled colors from memory, using a number of hand dyes to reproduce the soft images of the mountains, villages, and Inca ruins. *Lost in Time* is a very intuitive piece expressing the broad expanses and intense beauty of the continent, the cultural contrast of Spanish and South American Indian, the amazing acceptance of defeat by the Indians, and their mature adoption of and adaptation to the Spanish way. Remarkable! We have much to learn from the South Americans as we finally join the nations of the world and amble into the 21st century.

The interaction of colors, the contrast of textures, the relationships between shapes and lines—these formal elements of visual art, along with the reactions they elicit in the viewer, are aspects of quiltmaking which hold my interest.

Staccato 6 is one of a series of quilts which explore the energy and tension produced when stripes are pieced against stripes.

Ruth Garrison

Tempe, Arizona

Staccato 6
34″ x 34″

Cotton fabrics, poly-cotton batting, cotton thread

Screen printed, machine pieced, machine quilted

Keiko Goke

Sendai Miyagi, Japan

Logcabin in Wonderland II

60" x 61"

Cotton fabrics

Machine pieced and quilted

One of my favorite patterns is the log cabin, and I have been making them for a very long time. Most of my log cabin blocks are freehand cut, and the strips have been straight. However, last year when I attended Nancy Crow's workshop, she showed us how easy it was to sew curvilinear strips together, and ever since I sew nothing but curves!

This quilt honors the memory of my mother from whom I inherited my love of textiles; it honors my mentor friends, Rhoda Cohen, Nancy Halpern, and Matisse; it takes me back to my Brazilian roots and brings me into my own. Since making *Sewing by the Dining Table*, I have embarked on the exploration of small visual moments that happen indoors when rays of light hit a bowl of fruit, or outdoors when on a bleak winter day a very red cardinal rearranges my thinking.

Beatriz Grayson

Winchester, Massachusetts

Sewing by the Dining Table

31" x 36"

Commercial and hand-dyed fabrics

Machine pieced and quilted, hand appliquéd

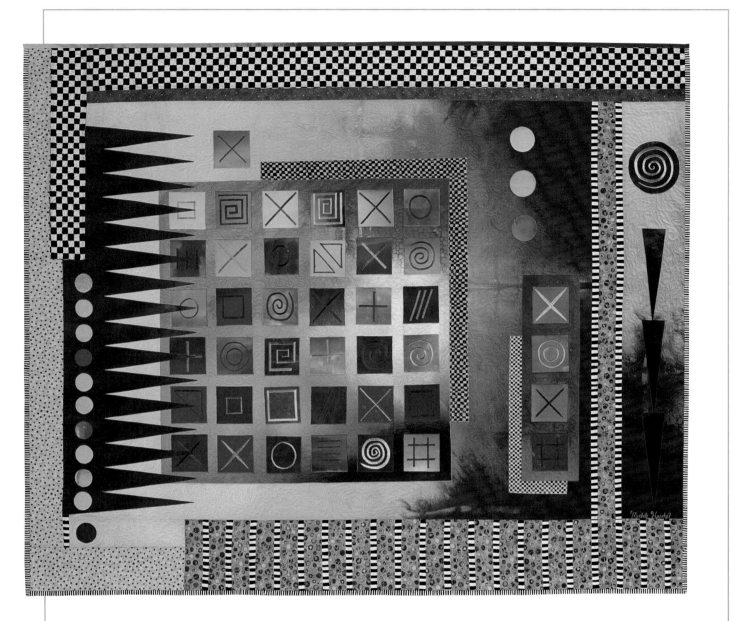

Michele Hardy

Mandeville, Louisiana

November Games

55″ x 45″

Cotton fabrics hand dyed by the quilter and other artists, commercial prints, rayon thread, cotton batting

Fused machine appliqué, machine pieced, machine embroidered, free-motion machine quilted

As the shorter, darker November days signal an abrupt end to summer, my focus is automatically shifted indoors to begin studio games. When I choose to play the game is of my own creation, with my own rules. Drawing from imagery and symbols of universally popular games, *November Games* is an expression of my artistic vision and commitment to fun, happy, spontaneous, colorful quilt art.

It is awesome to abstract an idea so no recognition of my inspiration is evident; instead, giving viewers the opportunity to make their own associations. Wouldn't it be fun to hear their musings? For this series, reflections are my fascination. We are all too often in a hurry to be aware of unique and changing designs. Work with my hand-dyed fabrics allows me to choose my unique palette.

Patty Hawkins

Lyons, Colorado

Basically Scribbles

48″ x 60″

Cotton fabric hand dyed by the artist, canvas

Machine pieced, discharge dyed, freehand cut, fused

Marilyn Henrion

New York, New York

Unless Something Happens
68" x 63.5"

Silk, cotton, linen, metallic fabrics

Machine pieced, hand appliquéd, hand quilted

This quilt was created upon returning from a visit to Russia in 1996. The title refers to the unpredictability of life in that country during this period of transition. In a typical encounter, when confronted with my question about a Moscow restaurant being closed the previous evening, despite its claim to be open seven days a week, the manager responded that they *are* open seven days a week "unless something happens." The motifs in this piece (cross in the circle and interlocking crosses) are found in many Russian icons, while the dissonance of contemporary Russian life is reflected in the juxtapositions of fabrics.

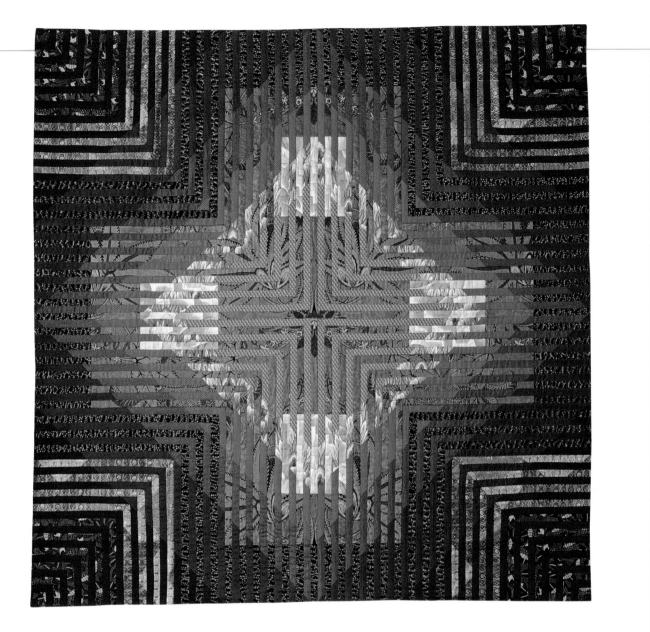

For many years I have been studying color progressions. I wonder how colors presented in a sequence can affect the eye and the heart, and how colors change each other because of the way they overlap. In *Box in the Diamond* I attempted to harmonize two geometric forms. I am always striving to create something beautiful, my only message being "Truth is Beauty." I am moved and inspired by music and nature.

Nancy Herman

Merion, Pennsylvania

Box in the Diamond

60″ x 60″

Cotton fabric

Machine pieced, machine appliquéd and quilted

Gretchen B. Hill

San Jose, California

La Mathrugada
53.25″ x 20.25″

Cotton fabric, rayon thread

*Machine pieced and quilted, dyed, painted,
overdyed and discharge dyed*

From my patio I have a beautiful view of the sun setting over the Santa Cruz Mountains. This has inspired me to pursue my fascination with the interplay of light and color at sunrise and sunset in a quilt series. My dyed fabrics are perfect to illustrate these natural phenomena.

Self-described as "eclectic," I don't follow any one system but instead chase my ideas and inspirations, exploiting any technique, which serves the purpose. This quilt is a successful response to my recent exploration with folded surfaces using the basic nature of a quilt. At rest, this quilt quietly folds up into its own box; on display, it rises triumphantly out of the box, unfolding 15 architecturally related pop-up scenes.

In one sudden moment I beheld the image of the finished piece in my mind. With a leap of faith, a bull-dog grip on perseverance, and no arbitrary boundaries on solutions to design or engineering problems, the quilt arrived. Color, texture, line, scale, pattern, and the balance between harmony and dissonance are the design elements which hold my attention, all of which were considered in this quilt.

Wendy Hill

Sunriver, Oregon

On the Street Where I Live
box 5″ x 5″ x 2″, quilt 4.5″ x 48″

Commercial hand-dyed cotton fabric, thread, fusible web, cardboard (for box), spray adhesive

Surface stitching, fusing, cut-outs, folding, functional stitching to hold layers together

Sue Holdaway-Heys

Ann Arbor, Michigan

Bee Balm

64" x 59"

Cotton fabrics dyed by the artist

Soft-edge appliqué, surface stitching, dry-brush fabric paint

Bee Balm is part of a series of art quilts in which I have "zoomed in" on a particular flower native to Michigan that grows in my large perennial garden. I am exploring the patterns and shapes created through contrast in value and color while also incorporating lots of surface texture with a variety of threads.

I'm continually amazed by the number of men that regularly go to watch lap dancers and keep this pastime a secret from their significant other. The research for this piece required many hours of watching the movies *Striptease*, *Showgirls*, and *Lap Dancers*—just to get the moves right.

Wendy C. Huhn

Dexter, Oregon

How Much Freedom Should a Wife Permit Her Husband?

29" x 46"

Cotton fabrics, batting, acrylic paint, phosphorescent medium, dimensional paint, monofilament thread

Photocopy fabric, heat transfers, heliographic printing, dextrin resist fabric, stencils, screen printing, hand stitched, machine quilted

Melody Johnson

Cary, Illinois

Parallel Paths

72.5″ x 47.75″

Hand-dyed cotton, fusible web, cotton batting, Madeira rayon embroidery thread, YLI Wonder thread

Fusible appliqué, machine pieced, machine quilted

Parallel Paths is the seventh in the *Cracked Pavement* series, inspired by the lyrical broken lines of aging streets and sidewalks. As the series progressed, it veered into mosaics, bricks, and stone walkways. Besides the play of color and contrast, I am most interested in the space between the stones and the supporting line of the design. Breaking up the composition into four panels hopefully moved it from the natural world into the abstract, referring to individuals sharing the same life paths, yet remaining distinct.

Solar Wind is the summer quilt in my botanically inspired *Calyx* series. As a native New Englander, I grew up with the heat, humidity, and blended colors of a typical summer day. Now living in the West, I find many summer days to be dry and often windy, causing the brightly defined colors to dance with vibrant neon energy.

Crane Johnson

Eagle, Idaho

Solar Wind

45″ x 45″

Cotton fabrics, holographic metallic threads

Machine pieced, hand quilted

Natasha Kemper-Cullen

Topsham, Maine

Chaos
48″ x 48″

Fiber-reactive dyes, textile inks, cotton fabrics, tulle, rayon and metallic threads

Printing methods: block, monoprints, monotypes, silk screen, cyanotype, brush and sponge; spatter painting, collage construction, machine stitched, hand quilted, beaded

At present there are seven pieces in the series I call *Saints and Sinners* which were inspired by a beautiful woven piece entitled *The Seven Saints* made by a friend of mine. The work he wove actually depicts eight figures, one of which has subtle differences which distinguish it visually from the other seven. I started thinking about how we are so quick to judge others by the first impression given by a person's attitude and appearance. Often we decide what a person is like based only on this superficial data.

We don't always give people enough time for us to find out what they are really like.

Chaos, like the other pieces in the series, explores on a very intuitive level some of the ramifications of this hasty assessing and judging we do. Each piece in the series contains some elements of some of the other panels while maintaining an integrity or theme of its own.

Marks left by generations past and by nature leave their legacy on this image of an ancient wall, speaking to the legends we pass on, a plea for remembrance, an input of our significance. Working with cloth is both a comfort and a challenge. It is tactile evidence that we were here and left something of value—a mirror of ourselves and our accomplishments.

Beth T. Kennedy

Austin, Texas

Legends of An Old Wall II

40" x 48.5"

Hand-dyed cotton, cotton embroidery thread, silk-screen ink, puff paint, beads, textured acrylic medium, paint, artist-made paper, oriental prayer papers

Hand-dye painted, silk screened, stamped, machine embroidered, machine quilted

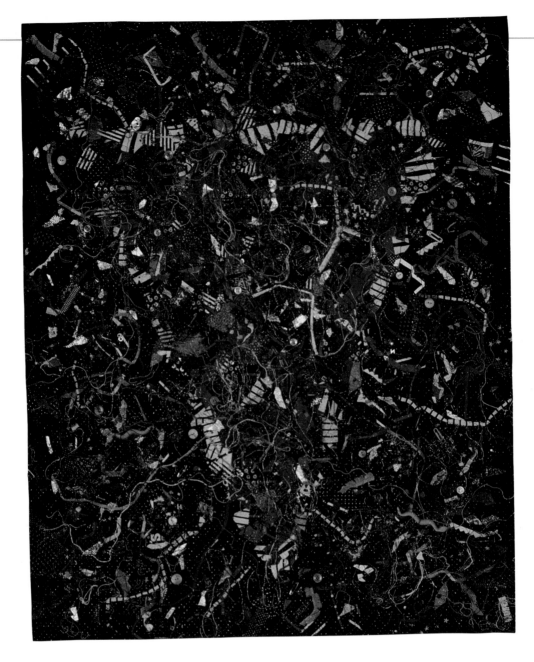

Pat Kroth

Verona, Wisconsin

Night Noise

30″ x 37″

Fiber fragments of cotton, blends, velvet, silk, tulle, lace and trims, and found objects such as toys, notions, safety pins, paper clips, thread, hardware, and buttons

Heat-bonded fiber fragments, tulle overlay, randomly machine stitched with rayon and cotton threads

Night Noise is from a series of quilting that uses a shield as a primary symbol. The inverted triangle or shield is recognizable to drivers and pedestrians in our culture as a warning sign. A shield in contemporary as well as medieval times refers to a shelter or protective covering. My "covering" in this instance includes the manipulation of fabric fragments fused and then entrapped, along with found objects, in a thin layer of fragile tulle.

I enjoy the visual interplay of hard and soft, logical and illogical, predetermined and random, shielded and unshielded.

I collect and incorporate items with interesting texture, color, or personal significance. I often think of my work as a depository for the flotsam and jetsam of life. *Night Noise* was titled late on a spring night while listening to spring peeper frogs against a background of improv jazz.

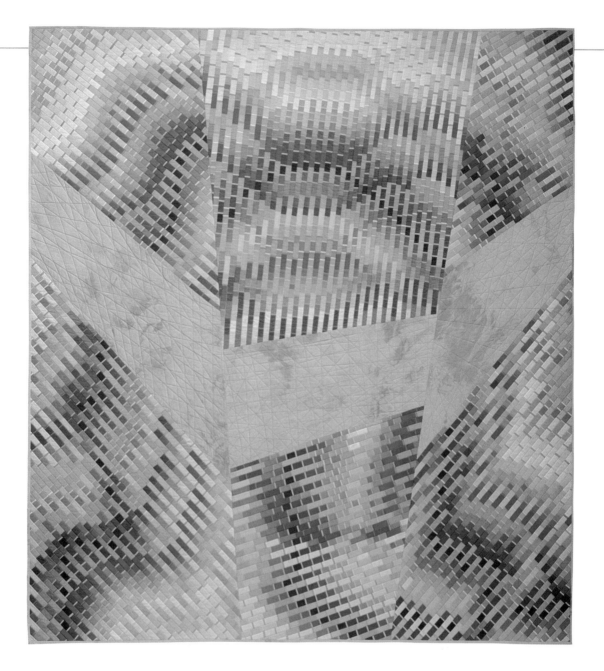

Starting in late November and continuing through Solstice into late January, the early mornings in Boston are pale and soft. I love these skies which I see every day that is clear on my way to work. I am compelled each year to do some work that incorporates these colors. I am otherwise very drawn to vivid and saturated hues. *January: Early Morning* is as close as I come to making a pictorial quilt. The FTDF fabrics enhance the soft color with their soft texture.

Judith Larzelere

Belmont, Massachusetts

January: Early Morning
69" x 76"

Fabric dyed by FTDF, cotton fabric, polyester batting

Machine strip pieced, machine strip quilted

Jocelyne LeRoy

Vendargues, France

Fisole

53″ x 53″

Cotton fabric

Machine pieced and quilted

I was so amazed by the beautiful colors of the hills surrounding Florence, Italy, that I wanted to put them in my quilt. Light and dark fabrics helped me play with the contrasts: day/night, winter/summer, shadow/sunlight in the four-part center of the blocks. Then I surrounded them with uneven stripes playing light against dark.

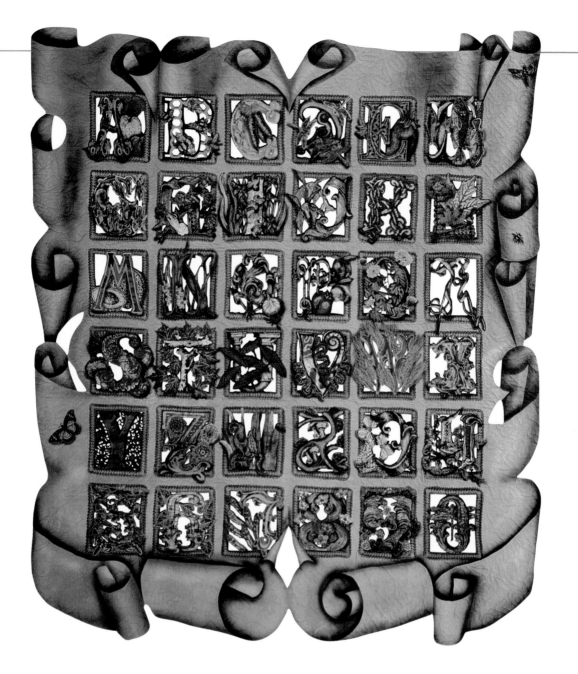

Every story begins with a letter. Each letter tells a story.

M. Joan Lintault

Carbondale, Illinois

Untitled

86″ x 97″

Cotton fabric, thread and batting

Dyed, screen printed, airbrushed, hand painted, computer-generated designs, appliquéd, quilted, sewing machine lace

Sharon Little

Santa Fe, New Mexico

Bless the Ties that Bind

77.5" x 77.5"

*Commercial cottons, old bow ties, silk,
monofilament and rayon threads*

Machine stitched, appliquéd, and quilted

Bless the Ties that Bind is in memory of George W. Pierson, whose family and friends perpetuated his fashion signature by giving him such a wonderful and diverse array of bow ties to wear.

George's daughter, Nora, and I collaborated on the quilt, which is a realization of her dream and will hang in the family's summer home.

Rookie Award Winner

Shapes and textures of old structures lend themselves to reinterpretation in fabric. I enjoy the challenge of creating the illusion of rustic wood and peeling paint through fabric and thread.

In rural Cartersville, Georgia, this weathered barn stands precariously by a creek on property belonging to my friend, Mary Hart. *Mary's Barn* is sixth in series of primitive doors, in each piece of which I've endeavored to preserve an image of the past,

Vita Marie Lovett

Marietta, Georgia

Primitive Door Series VI — Mary's Barn

19.25″ x 22″

Canvas, cotton, acrylic paint, cotton thread

Painted, machine thread painting, machine quilted

Terrie Hancock Mangat
Cincinnati, Ohio

Freedom Fire Works
96" x 88.5"

Cotton fabric, African tied dyed cottons, African mud cloth, hand-embroidered flowers from Oaxaca, Mexico, collaged paper, chenille pipe cleaners, African trade beads, cowry shells, Czech glass beads, antique beads, mirror cloth from India

Machine pieced, appliquéd, beaded, hand embroidered, hand quilted, painted with acrylic paint

I try to make a fireworks quilt every year after the end of summer celebration on the river. The whole visual image of the bursts of color against the changing sky fascinates me. The marks of the floating smoke from previous bursts are as important to the image as the current burst. I go home with the memory and impressions and gather together the various ingredients to make a new version of the celebration. This *Freedom Fire Works* is an expression of the recently felt freedom in my life.

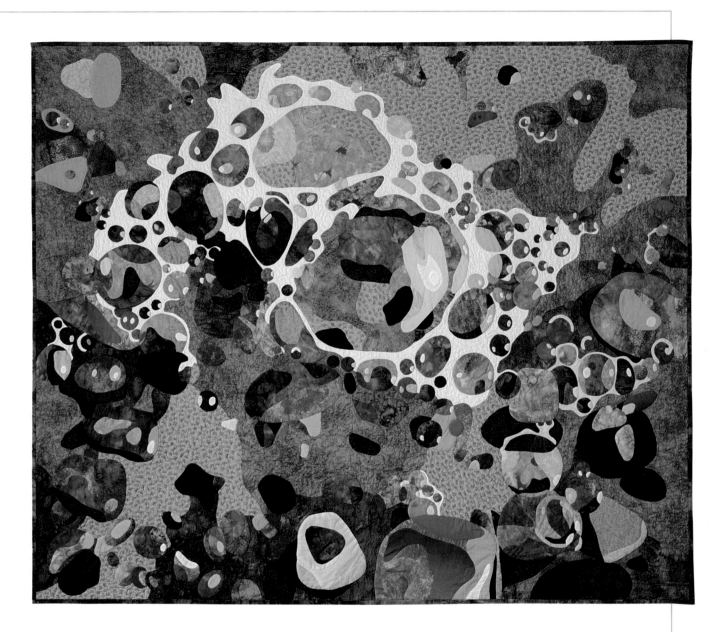

On a calm, sunny morning on the beach, at the water's edge. . . . Do you remember watching the busy glints from the sun as it is reflected randomly by the water, the wet pebbles, and the myriad of bubbles—all at a pace set by the small waves as they gently wash inward.

This contradiction of busy-ness reined by peace and tranquillity is fascinating. Even more fascinating is the fact that it is peace and tranquillity which stay with you long after you have returned to your busy city life in . . . well, for us, it is Paris!

This quilt was made to preserve this feeling a little longer. It allows us to refresh our memories and conveys this special mood to anyone who spends a minute or two in front of it.

Inge Mardal & Steen Hougs

Saint-Germain-En-Laye, France

Present Meets Past
54" x 45"

Cotton fabrics, batting

Hand appliquéd, machine quilted

Mary Mashuta

Berkeley, California

Trumpet Vine

59" x 59"

Cotton fabrics, among them a wide assortment of woven stripes that include some designed by Roberta Horton and Kaffe Fassett, handmade stripes and printed solids by Lunn Fabrics and Stacey Michelle

Machine pieced, machine quilted with monofilament and rayon threads

Stripes are my "thing." Two intense, full-fledged attempts to combine four colorways of one stripe with a collection of vegetable prints failed. A shoe box of cut "pieces that didn't work" later, I finally accepted that my quilt had chosen the direction it wanted to go and removed the offending vegetables and stripes. When I looked out my studio window, to my amazement I saw the trumpet vine and realized it contained the colors in my quilt.

Only two templates were used to create the original interlocking design, but this is a good example of the whole being more than the sum of its parts.

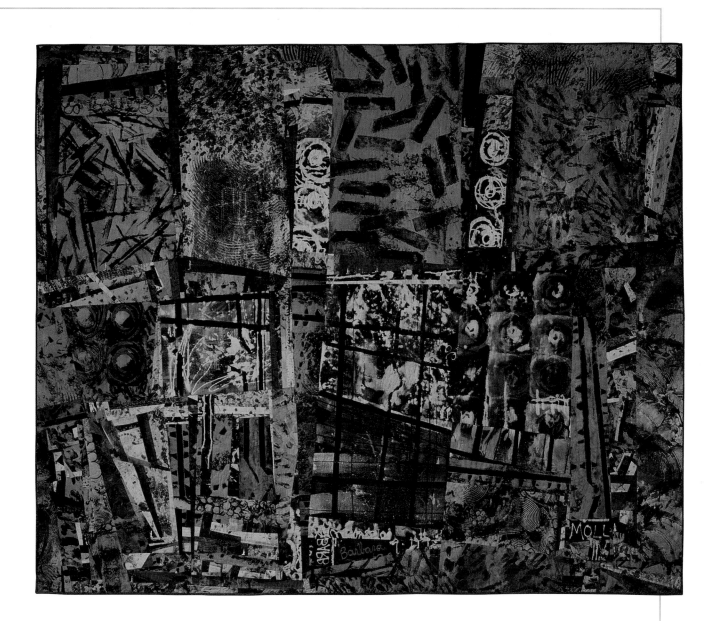

For over three years I have been working on a series of abstract quilts which deal with man's inhumanity to man, particularly with aspects of the bombing of Hiroshima. *When God Weeps* is my response to the following poem by Mildred Raynolds Trivers. The poem and the quilt were created for the Humpback Barn Festival of Poetry and Art in Muncie, Indiana.

God of History

God of Hiroshima and of Holocaust
God of History and of Oklahoma City
God of might, God of massacre
Terrible pitiless God
Whom we address as God of Mercy
Whom we preach as God of Love
Whom we serve as God of Hate.

On my knees! On my knees!

God of Job and of Golgotha!
Why hast Thou forsaken us?
Why has Thou led us and left us?
Under tons of bodies, under tons of bricks?
To what end? For what purpose
Do we dwell in the valleys of Horror?

On my knees! On my knees!

Barbara Moll

Muncie, Indiana

When God Weeps: Hiroshima Series

98" x 82"

Cotton fabric discharged with a variety of resist materials and bleach solutions

Machine pieced, hand quilted, embellished with Latin American milagros

Freddy Moran

Orinda, California

You're a Lifesaver

80" x 80"

Cotton fabrics

Machine pieced, machine quilted

What would happen if I made circles of bright colors on a field of bright colors? I would have made a quilt called *You're a Lifesaver*! My quilts are about color, fearlessly and joyfully used in profusion. I rarely know where the design is going when I begin, and I am often amazed with the finished quilt. This quilt started as a traditional design and became *You're a Lifesaver*.

My work focuses on women's issues. The quilt is my preferred medium because it reinforces the feminine context of my work and allows me to express my ideas better than any other medium. I apply color and imagery to fabrics by dyeing, discharge dyeing, painting, printing, and photocopying. These fabrics are then cut up, reassembled, and pieced. Using this fabric collage method, I am able to combine fabrics and images to give my work a sense of depth, spontaneity, and revolution.

Hidden Agenda explores the veiled issues in love, relationships, and seduction.

Cynthia Myerberg

Morgantown, West Virginia

Hidden Agenda
40" x 54"

Cotton fabric, silk organza, hand-dyed cotton

Discharge dyed, hand dyed, xerox transfer, machine pieced, machine quilted, tied

Paula Nadelstern

Bronx, New York

Kaleidoscope XVI:
More is More

64″ x 64″

Cotton and silk fabric

Machine pieced, hand quilted

An unexpected consequence of my interest in making kaleidoscope quilts is my friendship with kaleidoscope makers. At first I was so bewitched by their handiwork, I assumed they were either geniuses or wizards. Gradually, I began to decode the technical stuff behind the magic, and I found the artistry.

Inspiration for the intricate 12-sided, off-centered mandalas came from a kaleidoscope by Charles Karadimos, while the small scopes bordering the quilt are evocative of the interior images created by scope makers Bob and Sue Rioux. They are sprinkled with silk to simulate the glow of dichroic glass, a substance invented for the space program that shows different colors depending on the angle of light falling on it.

The result is a quilt comprised of layer after layer of uninhibited colors tumbling irrepressibly into unpredictable harmony.

This quilt is a continuation of my *Interweave Series* started in January 1983 with *Lattice Interweave*, perhaps my best-known quilt. I have been interested all my life in repetition of patterns and in illusions of depth. I have no real depth perception because my eyes don't achieve normal fusion because one eye is nearsighted and the other is farsighted.

I grew up in Pittsburgh, Pennsylvania. My father, an engineer, was interested in bridges, of which there are a great many in my hometown. During our frequent car trips, my Dad liked to show me the differences in their structures.

Several times over the years I have thought that my *Interweave Series* was finished. To my surprise, a new variation pops up to demand my attention. I designed this quilt three years before I made it. It took that long to figure out the construction problems and to learn the necessary airbrush techniques.

Miriam Nathan-Roberts
Berkeley, California

Fiber Dance
61″ x 57″

Cotton fabrics

Dyed, air brushed, machine pieced, appliquéd, and quilted

Anne McKenzie Nickolson

Indianapolis, Indiana

Give and Take

57″ x 68″

Cotton fabric

Machine pieced, hand appliquéd through all layers

My interest in reverse appliqué goes back about 20 years, when I first explored the possibilities in small hand-stitched pieces. The process of subtraction in order to allow a form to emerge is fascinating to me. What refreshed this interest was learning to design on the computer and finding that I could build a piece, cut away shapes, and subtract them, simulating the reverse-appliqué process. Though it is a more complex plan than I could have envisioned with my own brain, this design is only the basic plan for the finished quilt. There are many surprises and challenges. It has been my joy to watch the forms dance as each strip is stitched in place. It is only then that I can see if my plans have been successful in creating a complex and satisfying composition.

During the construction of this piece, I spent a great deal of time pondering my development and direction as a fiber artist.

Constance Norton

Fairfax, Virginia

Evolution

38″ x 44″

Cotton fabrics, cotton batting

Machine pieced and quilted

Ellen Oppenheimer

Oakland, California

C Block #3

47″ x 47″

Fabric, ink

Silk screened, machine pieced, machine quilted

When I was printing fabric for my *Labyrinth Series*, I always did my first screen on a piece of test fabric. To save fabric, I tried to use one piece of fabric for several test prints. As the layers of pattern grew on some of my test prints, I began to realize that they were interesting. The *C Block Series* is my attempt to capture what was fascinating in some of the test prints.

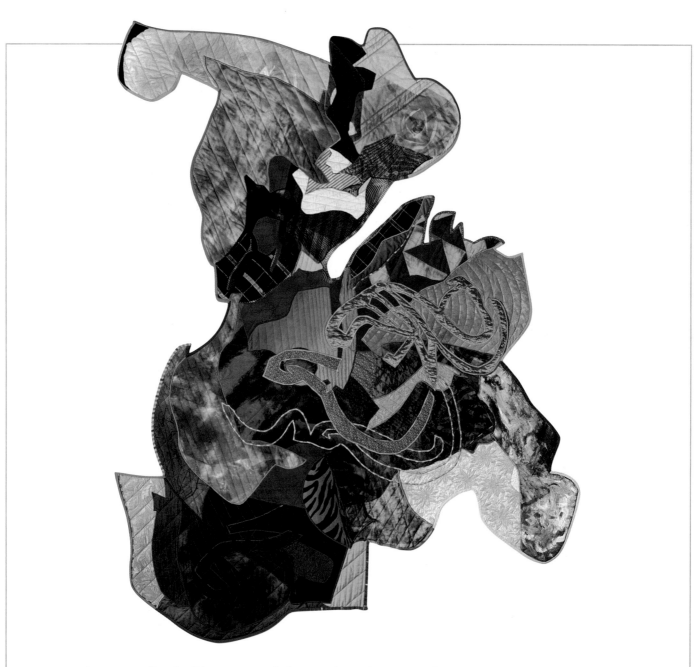

Cacafuego means "spitfire," but to my mind, the Spanish term has a more humorous cast. I love the humanity of this piece, its assertiveness, foolishness, and variety.

Five years ago, I began a series of "falling angel" quilts. Based on human forms, emotions, and movements, they became my personal rogues' gallery. Through them I explore desire, confusion, boredom, haste, etc.

Cacafuego is the anger quilt. I began with the clutched red fist and abdominal area which is the first connection with anger in my own body. As I worked, various aspects of anger became apparent; I could see the overwhelming feeling, the silly self-involvement, the manufactured words, and the cruelty of it. But I also saw anger sounding the alarm. "Wake up! Something is wrong!" I began almost to hear this piece.

Kathleen O'Connor

Putney, Vermont

Falling Angel — Cacafuego
67" x 93"

Hand-painted and -dyed cotton and silk fabric, commercial fabric, acrylic paint, cotton and rayon thread, batting

Machine appliquéd and pieced, hand dyed and painted

Katie Pasquini-Masopust

Santa Fe, New Mexico

Passage – Chaco

45" x 69"

Cotton, satin, lamé, blend fabrics, wool batting

Machine appliquéd, machine quilted

Penny Nii Art Quilt Award Winner

Passages – Chaco was taken from a photograph of the perfectly lined-up doors at the Chaco Canyon Monument in New Mexico. The Anasazi Indians lived there centuries ago and, without any modern tools, made these incredible doorways, all with 90-degree angles lined up one after the other for ventilation and wonderful optical illusions. I have been working on a series of *Passages*. This quilt has the actual passage through the doorways, but also a passage through the colored rectangles I added to give life to the gray structure. There is a ghost layer of bricks that floats in and out of the main structure. This is a culmination of the many passages I have gone through in my life to get to the wonderful place I am now.

I wanted to call this quilt *Full Circle*. In 1992, while visiting the San Blas Islands, Panama, I showed a Kuna woman a picture of my new quilt. Two years later, while visiting the same island, I bought a mola that I was 95 percent sure had been inspired by that quilt. It had the same X-shape motif repeated. The Kuna women quickly absorb outside stimulation. In 1997 I received a book on Kuna molas from Japan. This book has several variations I consider to be distant cousins of that original mola. One of them caught my eye and gave me an idea for using striped fabrics to form the same motif, which had been done as appliqué. I loved the supposition that I gave another culture an idea and then borrowed it back in a new way.

Charlotte Patera

Grass Valley, California

In and Out
58.5″ x 58.5″

Cotton fabrics, hand dyed and commercial

Machine pieced and quilted

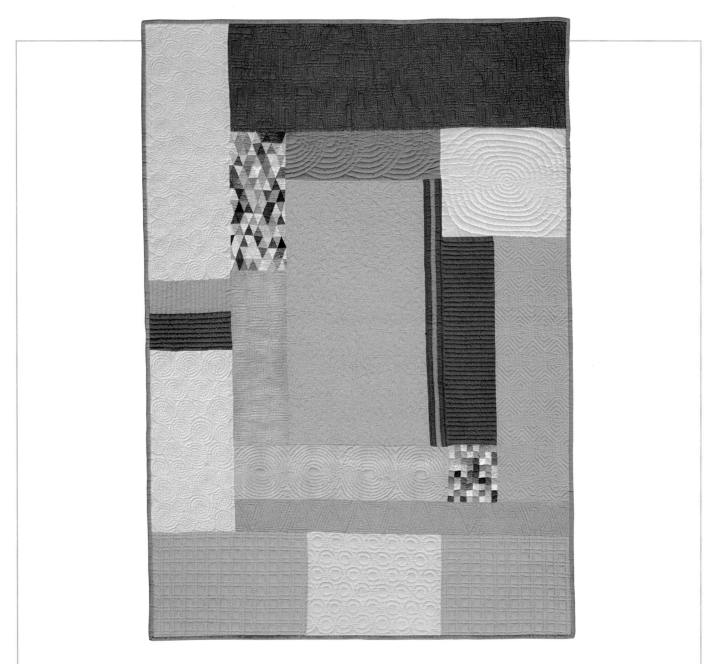

Karla Price

Miami, Florida

Textures
33″ x 45″

Cotton fabrics

Hand pieced, hand quilted

I am fascinated with printed fabrics that look as if they each have a unique feel.

My goal for this quilt was to create real texture that could actually be felt with the fingers. My challenge was to do the quilting without markings. It was a very freeing experience to let my fingers create the different patterns and to let my mind explore the lines and shapes.

The log cabin block has long been a symbol of hearth and home. For me, this interpretation represents the positive and negative created by keeping mind, body, and soul together while caring for ourselves and our families.

Wendy Richardson

Brooklyn Park, Minnesota

...Home Fires Burning
62" x 84"

Cotton fabrics overdyed by the artist

Machine and hand sewn, machine quilted

Jan Rickman

Whitewater, Colorado

Close Encounter

83.5″ x 47.5″

Cotton fabric hand dyed by the artist, rayon thread

Appliquéd, fused appliquéd, free-motion machine embroidery embellished and free-motion machine quilted

President's Choice Award Winner

Our planet is getting smaller and smaller, and the homes of many creatures are shrinking too. We need to be cognizant of the impact we each have on this planet. This work shows in detail two peaceful creatures; their random close encounter with each other is one of harmony.

Perhaps this piece will remind us of the harmonious close encounters we should have with all creatures and also remind us of our responsibility to nature.

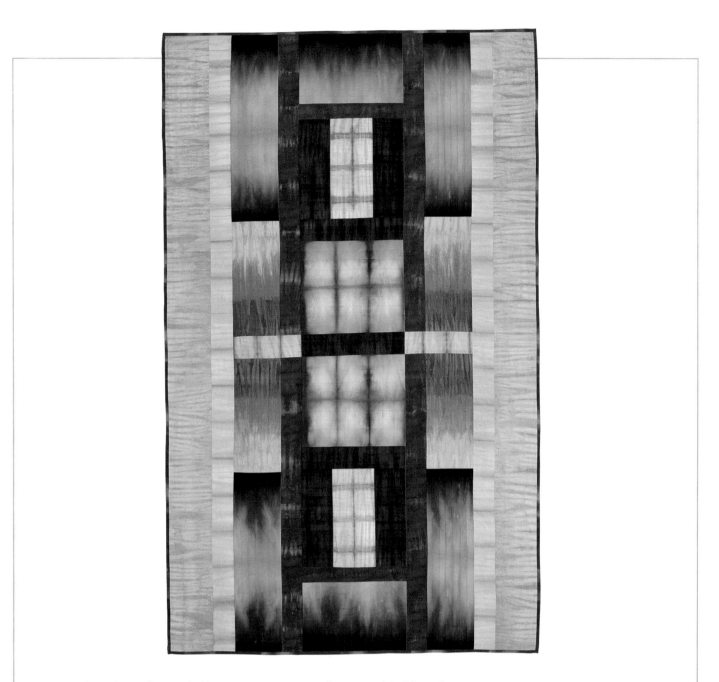

Colors often reflect and affect our emotions. From "mourners black" to "sunshine yellow," we clothe our bodies and furnish our homes. Naturally, our feelings are expressed through our art as well. The fiber medium very generously affords us this indulgence.

Excited by the vast possibilities, I began creating original fabric to incorporate in my quilts. *Brights I* is made with cotton fabric hand dyed with fiber-reactive dyes, using various shibori techniques.

At the time *Brights I* was designed, I realized that our dreams can be created, and I was feeling a tremendous sense of freedom without boundaries. As *Brights I* took form, I discovered several windows and even a ladder starting to emerge.

Working intuitively, I willingly relinquished much of the control to the medium, becoming not only a participant but also an observer.

Lauren Rosenblum

Forest Hills, New York

Brights I
42″ x 67.5″

Cotton fabrics, Procion dyes

Hand-dyed fabrics using tie-dye and shibori techniques, machine pieced, hand quilted

Bernie Rowell

Candler, North Carolina

Hundertwasser's Blue Forest

40" x 64"

Latex enamels on canvas, metallic fabrics and thread, vinyl, beads, ribbon

Painted canvas with sewn construction, embroidered, appliquéd, bonded, layered, collaged, hand-tied and machine-tacked quilting

My current landscape series is inspired by two things: moving to the mountains of western North Carolina and an ongoing interest in the work of Austrian painter Hundertwasser.

Hundertwasser's use of color and spiral forms was perfect for a sewn interpretation.

By using cartoon-like simplifications of flowers and leaves, I am attempting to express the creative energy, excitement, and sheer joy of life.

Jane A. Sassaman

Chicago, Illinois

Flower Field

54" x 42"

Commercial and hand-dyed cotton fabric, sheer and metallic synthetic fabric, cotton batting

Machine appliquéd, machine quilted

Susan Schapira

Anchorage, Alaska

Summer Mandala

31″ x 31″

Cotton hand-dyed by the artist, embroidery and shisha work from India, beads

Machine reverse appliqué, machine quilted

The mandala is a focus for meditation or for any ritual striving to manifest one's spirituality in everyday life. This mandala is formed from fragments of old Indian embroidery and shisha work, together with reverse appliqué designs which emphasize the embroidery patterns. Rivers run on the diagonal, showing the vitality and creativity which flow through our lives.

I have done a series of river rock quilts using a method that I am very comfortable with. That series has evolved into a series of foliage quilts. This is the first quilt in that series. The exploration of this concept can lead me in many directions, and I look forward to that exploration.

Connie Scheele

Houston, Texas

Foliage 1

40″ x 40″

Hand-dyed cotton fabric, cotton batting, silk quilting threads

Machine pieced, hand quilted

Carol Sara Schepps

Princeton Junction, New Jersey

Hammers

43.5″ x 30″

Cotton fabric, cotton batting

Constructed using Katie Pasquini-Masopust's fractured landscape technique, machine pieced and quilted

When I was little, I asked my father what he did at work. "Play with my little red hammer," he'd say. Both my father and my husband have a lot of tools, some old and cherished favorites, some new and waiting to be broken in. The personality of tools—their age, stance, composition, and character—has always held an interest for me.

The right tool for the job. The right medium for the creative. Years of art schooling . . . paint, pen, pencil, film for graphic design, fabric for fashion design. Imagine my surprise two years ago when I discovered fabric could be a tool to express all that I saw. *My* way of seeing could now be shared with family, friends, and strangers because I "discovered" that fabric could be a tool for my expression.

Hammers was inspired by a photograph by Eduardo Fuss.

I find inspiration for my quilts not in nature's majesty—mountains, waterfalls, glaciers—but in her more humble forms. Here, two Japanese maples in my neighbor's yard seem to form a radiant chorus line in October, Wisconsin's most glorious month. The leaves, trees, and foreground shrubbery are "cut-outs" from my vast array of printed cottons which I machine appliquéd to the background fabric. Then I machine quilted the piece within an inch of its life. This technique allows me almost as much spontaneity as painting, and I often create a fabric scene with neither a plan nor a photograph to guide me. I choose fabrics for my landscapes that have a wide variety of light and dark so that I can play as nature does, with light and shadow across the landscape of my quilt.

Natalie Sewell

Madison, Wisconsin

Dancing Maples

62.5 x 42"

Cotton fabrics, cotton thread, monofilament thread

Raw-edge machine appliqué, machine quilted

Fran Skiles

Plantation, Florida

Yalaha I
72" x 54"

Cotton duck, nylon tulle, woven hemp, thread, acrylic paint

Photo silk screen, color copy transfer, direct paint, machine appliquéd, machine pieced, machine quilted

The images in *Yalaha* are personal. They were taken from my property in Central Florida.

The very essential and characteristic way I work is to paint and create a layer on fabric, then regard it as a completely fresh ground by cutting, stitching, and painting—and repeating the process again and again. Working with free-hanging fabric allows me to experiment with raw edges, texture, and shape.

I never know when an image or concept will choose me. Visually attuned, camera in hand, I am beckoned. With pleasure and surprise, life's visual offerings are collected.

Beyond the consideration of formalistic design, I cannot say how the layering of these visual elements synergistically creates labyrinths of meaning. That is revealed when the newly formed image resonates. The mood may be sunny or dark, but somehow between desire and fulfillment falls my shadow at the Daimon's Cave.

Arlé Sklar-Weinstein

Hastings-on-Hudson, New York

Shadow at the Daimon's Cave

42.5" x 56"

Satin fabric, poly/cotton batting, rayon and nylon thread

Computer assisted image, heat transferred in 36 panels to satin fabric, after printing directly onto transfer paper panels are pieced and treated as a wholecloth quilt

Connie Stark

Toledo, Ohio

Sanctuary

49″ x 43″

Hand-dyed cotton fabric, metallic cording, metallic thread

Shibori dyed, machine pieced, machine quilted, machine couched thread

The circular and linear patterns produced with Japanese shibori dyeing were intriguing to me, and I became interested in producing fabric that would become the garden in my mind. The stitched and tied resist lines created the flowers and stems of my imaginary garden. The making of this quilt became my sanctuary for several months, providing tremendous joy and contentment.

The landscape in the north of Germany inspired me to make this quilt. I used hundreds of different fabrics in my crazy technique and worked in tiny small strips, so it looks like grass.

Dorle Stern-Straeter

Muenchen, Germany

Nordic Impressions
46.5″ x 50.5″

Cotton and silk fabric, hand-painted silk fabric

Crazy patch technique, machine pieced

Heide Stoll-Weber

Frankfurt, Germany

Forest Fire
56″ x 84″

Hand-dyed cottons by the artist

Machine pieced, machine quilted

Burning flowers, sulfur smoke, shadowy blues, mysterious greens, all to be found on narrow and wide strips of hand-dyed fabrics from my own dye studio. This quilt made itself within an ecstatic weekend session.

Looking across Similk Bay to Deception Pass State Park, Douglas firs create a jagged line against the sky. Up close, the giants show their age: long, barren trunks, branches missing and broken off, gruff statues soaring to the clouds. Gray northwest clouds reveal the rough contours. Salal, another native, thrives in their protection.

Old-growth Douglas fir trees can reach 125 feet in height with a canopy of only 25 feet, a ratio of 5:1. Up to half the tree can be barren of branches.

For my quilts I focus on an element of my surroundings that excites me. I study it through observation, drawing, and photography until I can capture its impression.

My purpose is to compare experiences with the viewer—a shared response, an observation taken for granted, a nuance not before realized.

Heather W. Tewell

Anacortes, Washington

Old Growth and Salal

89" x 61"

Cotton fabrics, cotton thread, cotton batting

Machine pieced, machine quilted

Michele Vernon

Falls Church, Virginia

Intersections #9
71" x 63"

Cotton fabric, hand-dyed fabrics by Michele Duell, acrylic-painted cotton

Machine pieced and quilted

I have been working on quilts that have a map theme for years. Issues of city planning and land use are in the back of my mind while designing the *Intersections* series. The focus of the series has been on where streets cross and the overall pattern they make. After all, intersections are where the action is. *Intersections #9* was designed on a slightly larger scale than earlier pieces to accommodate varied "road" widths and greater density in the center of the "city." In the space between the roads, life is lively and colorful.

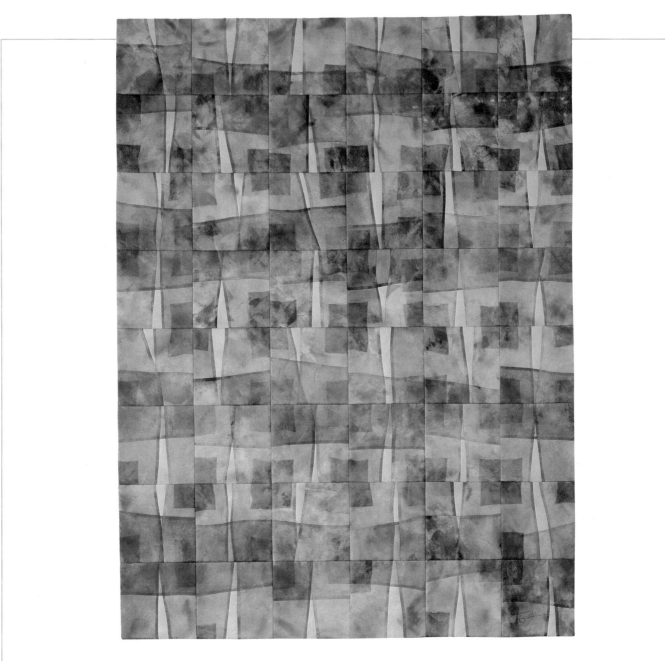

This is my third quilt using acrylic-painted canvas but my first time using acrylic-painted silk. My interpretation of the work and its title came to me after I finished the piece—when I became an observer, no longer absorbed in the creative process. To me, this quilt is about "the self" revealing itself; the inner light which we all have, but which we do not fully express because of inhibitions, beliefs, fears, or some other barrier. Still, that inner light is evident in varying degrees.

Nelda Warkentin

Anchorage, Alaska

The Self
48″ x 64″

Cotton canvas, silk, acrylic paint

Painted on silk and squares of painter's canvas, machine appliquéd and quilted through multiple layers

Susan Kendig Willen

Redondo Beach, California

The Lives of Women II: Maelstrom

57" x 50"

Cotton fabrics

Machine pieced using foundation paper piecing, hand quilted

As I move through my daily routine—at the gym, at my children's school, at the local coffee bar—I listen to the stories women have to tell. The stories haunt me (I cannot forget them) and I began the series *The Lives of Women* to share what I have heard: sadness, frustration, anger, humor, hope, courage, and resilience.

The image of the maelstrom is central to this second quilt in the series. It seems to me to be an apt metaphor both for the daunting forces with which women must contend and for our inner turmoil in the face of contradictory demands and changing expectations.

the community quilts

Since the opening of Visions: Quilts of a New Decade in 1990 at the Museum of San Diego History, Quilt San Diego has provided a Community Quilt to enhance the quilting experience of the public.

The quilts have been designed and constructed by local quilt artists and mounted on a quilting frame. The quilt and frame are then placed at the Museum, and the public is invited to quilt on the quilt during their visit to the exhibition. The community quilts have always been a popular addition to the exhibition.

Diamond Jubilee

75" x 92"

1990

Designed by Donalene H. Rasmussen, constructed by the quilters of San Diego under the direction of Donalene H. Rasmussen, quilted by visitors to *Visions: Quilts of a New Decade.* From the collection of the Museum of San Diego History.

Designed and constructed by Carol McKee Manning, quilted by visitors to *Visions: The Art of the Quilt.* From the collection of Quilt San Diego.

Our Pretty Planet
95" x 95"
1992

Layers of Excellence

116" x 96"

1994

Designed and constructed by Christen Brown and Julia Zgliniec using blocks provided by the artists of *Visions: Layers of Excellence* which portrayed their quilt entry, quilted by the visitors to *Visions: Layers of Excellence.* From the collection of Quilt San Diego.

94

Designed and constructed by Marie Fritz, Stevii Graves, Sharon Harris, Janeene Herchold, Mary Hjalmarson, Jan Rashid, Donna Rasmussen, Gay Sinclair, Patty B. Smith and Carolyn Zondler. Quilted by the visitors to *Visions: Quiltart*. From the collection of Quilt San Diego.

Wish You Were Here
60″ x 74″
1996

The Artists

The Quilts